The Really **Wild Life** of **Insects**™

ASSASSIN BUGS

ANDREW HIPP

The Rosen Publishing Group's
PowerKids Press™
New York

MID-CONTINENT PUBLIC LIBRARY

3 0000 12319622 6

For Virginia Kline

Published in 2003 by The Rosen Publishing Group, Inc.
29 East 21st Street, New York, NY 10010

First Edition

Editor: Gillian Houghton
Book Design: Mike Donnellan, Michael de Guzman

Photo Credits: Cover, back cover, p. 12 © Doug Wechsler/Animals Animals; p. 4 © Richard La Val/Animals Animals; p. 7 © G. W. Willis/Animals Animals; p. 8 © James H. Robinson/Animals Animals; pp. 11, 19 © Gallo Images/CORBIS; p. 11 (inset) © Michael Fogden/Animals Animals; p. 12 (inset) © Raymond A. Mendez/Animals Animals; p. 15 © Dennis Sheridan; p. 16 © Frank Lane Picture Agency/CORBIS; p. 20 © Robert and Linda Mitchell.

Hipp, Andrew.
Assassin bugs / by Andrew Hipp.
p. cm. — (The really wild life of insects)
Includes bibliographical references (p.   ).
Summary: Introduces the assassin bug, which pounces on victims, poisons .them, and sucks them dry.
ISBN 0-8239-6240-7 (lib. bdg.)
1. Assassin bugs—Juvenile literature. [1. Assassin bugs.] I. Title.
  QL523.R4 H56 2003
  595.7'54—dc21

                                                                    2001005447

Manufactured in the United States of America

CONTENTS

FUN FACTS
SOME ASSASSIN BUGS
HAVE STICKY PADS ON
THEIR LEGS FOR
CATCHING SMOOTH-
SHELLED INSECTS.

ASSASSIN BUGS

Deadly **assassin** bugs live in fields and forests all over the world. Some **species** of assassin bug wait, **camouflaged** in flowers, for their prey to approach. Other species stalk their prey on the ground. When an assassin bug finds a tasty insect, the assassin bug leaps forward and uses its spined or sticky forelegs to grab the insect. The assassin bug plunges its beak into its prey and pumps poison into the insect. The poison kills the insect and turns its organs into liquid. The assassin bug sucks out its prey's insides through its strawlike beak, sometimes feeding for more than an hour to get every tasty drop.

Many kinds of assassin bugs are brightly colored, alerting insect hunters that they are dangerous.

WHAT IS A BUG?

Assassin bugs form one family within the insect **order** Hemiptera. Entomologists, the scientists who study insects, use the name "bug" only for insects of the order Hemiptera. All other insects are simply called insects. As do most insects, bugs have two pairs of wings. Their front wings are light and papery thin at the tips, which makes them good for flying. Unlike other insects, the front wings of bugs are thick and leathery at the base, making the wings strong. These divided wings give the order its scientific name. *Hemi* comes from a Greek word meaning "half," and *ptera* comes from the Greek word for "wings."

The white spots and the yellow stripes on this white spot assassin bug might be a warning to enemies to watch out!

FUN FACTS
THEIR WINGS CAN GIVE
BUGS UNUSUAL
APPEARANCES. SOME
BUGS' WINGS OVERLAP
TO LOOK LIKE A LARGE X.

FUN FACTS
MOSQUITOES,
BUTTERFLIES, MOTHS,
LICE, BEES, AND FLEAS
ALL HAVE LONG,
SUCKING MOUTHPARTS.

AN UNUSUAL BEAK

All bugs have a strong, tube-shaped **proboscis**, or beak. The proboscis contains two long, wiry parts called **stylets**, which are used for piercing and for cutting. A protective **labium**, or lip, is wrapped around the stylets. A bug uses its labium like a tongue to taste the surface of its food. To feed, the bug jabs its needle-sharp stylets into its prey or a plant. There are two slender canals inside the stylets. The bug squirts out **saliva** through one canal. The saliva breaks down the food, turning it into a liquid. When its food has been turned into juice, the bug sucks it up through the other stylet canal.

This assassin bug will withdraw its beak and will clean itself before searching for another meal.

BLOODSUCKERS

One of the most famous kinds of assassin bugs is the kissing bug. Kissing bugs live in warm climates all over the world. Many species live in thatch roofs and in cracks in walls during the day. At night they come out of hiding and suck the blood of humans or other animals. They can drink 10 times their own weight in blood at one feeding. These insects are called kissing bugs because many species sting people on their faces, sometimes leaving painful sores. Other species live in the nests of small animals. These kissing bugs suck the blood of their animal hosts.

A bed bug, a relative of the kissing bug, prepares to suck human blood. An assassin bug (inset) feasts on a grasshopper.

▶

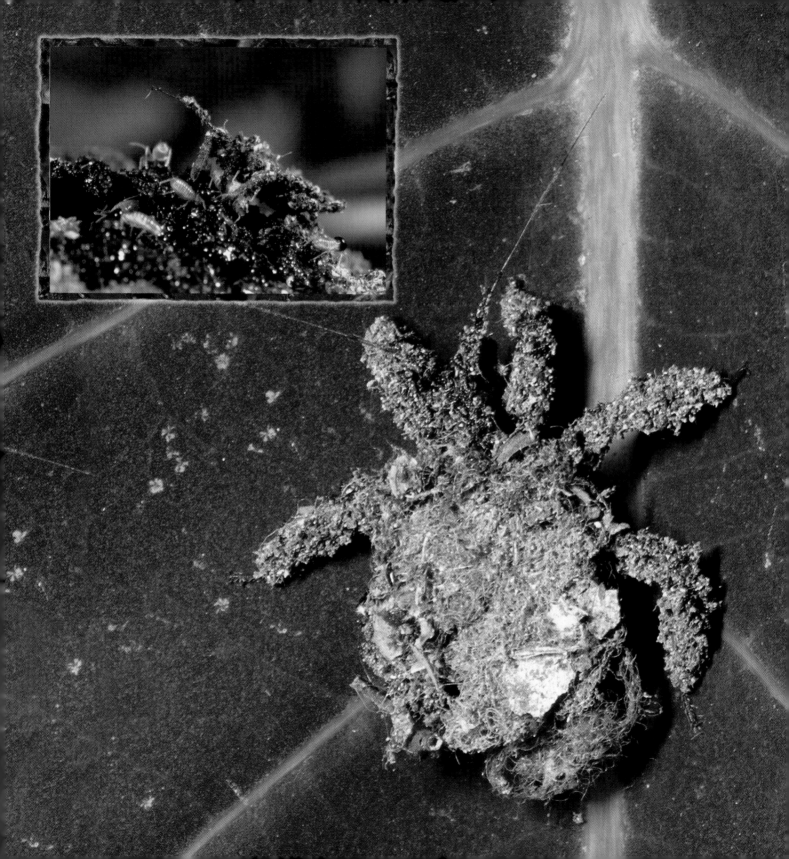

YOUNG ASSASSINS

Assassin bugs undergo **incomplete metamorphosis**. The young **nymphs** are like small adults in their appearance, but the nymphs lack wings. Assassin bug nymphs usually live in the same surroundings as their parents and eat similar foods. Nymphs of some species look like ants or mantids, both of which are dangerous insect hunters. This likeness scares off some insects that might hunt the nymphs. Nymphs of other species, such as the masked hunter, camouflage themselves in a peculiar way. They cover themselves with dust, leaves, or the shells of dead insects. Sticky hairs hold these bits of natural waste in place on the nymphs' backs.

These assassin bug nymphs have covered themselves with dust and leaves. As adults they will be hidden by their coloring.

13

As an assassin bug nymph grows, it becomes too big for its **exoskeleton**, or shell. A new exoskeleton grows underneath the old one. Then the old exoskeleton cracks open. The soft, moist assassin bug crawls out. The bug waits for several minutes or hours while the new exoskeleton hardens in the air and becomes strong. An assassin bug nymph molts, or sheds, its shell five times before becoming a full-grown adult with wings and the **reproductive organs** that it will need to mate.

Adult assassin bugs search for mates, or partners, using sound, smell, and sight. Mates approach each other slowly and often touch **antennae** before mating.

A newly molted assassin bug is in danger of being hurt as it waits for its wings and exoskeleton to harden in the air.

FUN FACTS

A MALE ASSASSIN BUG
SOMETIMES STEALS A
FEMALE'S FOOD WHILE
SHE IS EATING IT.

FUN FACTS
AN ASSASSIN BUG
NYMPH'S WINGS BEGIN
AS TINY, FLIGHTLESS
WING PADS ON THE
OUTSIDE OF ITS BODY.

EGGS

After mating, an assassin bug female lays her eggs. She lays them on a plant stem, in the ground, on the soil surface, or under rocks. She might lay her eggs singly or in groups of 150 or more, depending on the species. In some species, the male or the female guards the eggs and fights off **predators** and **parasites** until the eggs hatch. Laying many eggs in one place makes the eggs easier to guard.

Assassin bug eggs look like barrels with caps on the tops. About 10 days to several months after an egg is laid, the baby inside pushes the top open and wriggles out of the egg. Its exoskeleton hardens in the open air, and the nymph goes in search of food.

The eggs of this shieldbug, which is also in the order Hemiptera, will hatch two or three weeks after they are laid.

COMMON SCENTS

Glands are organs in the body that collect, make, and release chemicals. Bugs are born with glands that produce strong chemicals. Some of these chemicals have a horrible smell, giving one group of bugs the name stinkbugs. Their smell may sting a predator's eyes or scare it off. Other glands produce chemicals that kill harmful **bacteria**.

Some kinds of parasites have learned to find bugs by following the smell of the chemicals that the bugs make. These parasites lay their eggs inside of bugs. When they hatch, the baby parasites feed on the bug's organs. Over time they chew their way through the bug's exoskeleton, usually leaving the bug dead.

The unpleasant smell produced by special glands give stinkbugs like this one their names.

FUN FACTS
ONE GROUP OF ASSASSIN
BUGS USES DEAD
TERMITES AS BAIT TO
ATTRACT CURIOUS
TERMITE WORKERS.

FISHING FOR PREY

Assassin bugs also use chemicals as bait. Some assassin bugs collect sticky plant juices on their bodies. These juices smell good to insects, who fly right into the assassin bug's spiny legs. One kind of assassin bug is able to spit a stream of poisonous saliva at prey up to 12 inches (30 cm) away. Another kind of assassin bug makes a sweet-smelling poison in glands on its **abdomen**. Bright yellow or red hairs on its abdomen become coated with the poison. The bug walks to an ant trail, where ants lick the sweet hairs. Soon the ants become paralyzed, or unable to move. The bug slips its beak into a live ant and begins to feed.

Assassin bug nymphs gather on a fragrant flower and wait for the insects that will be drawn to the flower's sweet-smelling juices.

ASSASSIN BUGS AND PEOPLE

Assassin bugs, along with other predatory insects, hunt many insect pests. Farmers and gardeners like assassin bugs, because they kill many of the insects that feed on and lay eggs in plants. Farmers use them to control insect populations in soybean and cotton fields. Nature lovers like watching assassin bugs hunt their prey.

You can look for assassin bugs in shrubs, in grasslands, in forests, and even in gardens. Remember that assassin bugs use their strong bites in self-defense. If you go looking for assassin bugs, be careful. Use a net, not your hands, to capture them.

GLOSSARY

abdomen (AB-duh-min) The large, rear section of an insect's body.

antennae (an-TEH-nee) Thin, rodlike organs on the heads of insects that are used for smelling and feeding. The singular form is antenna.

assassin (uh-SA-sin) An expert killer.

bacteria (bak-TEER-ee-uh) Tiny living things that can be seen only with a microscope. Some bacteria cause illness or decay, while others are helpful.

camouflaged (KA-muh-flahjd) Made to blend into one's surroundings.

exoskeleton (ek-soh-SKEH-leh-tin) The harder outer shell of an insect's body.

incomplete metamorphosis (in-kum-PLEET meh-tuh-MOR-fuh-sis) The series of minor changes that an insect undergoes when it changes from nymph to adult, resulting in an increase in size but not a great change in form.

labium (LAY-bee-um) A lip. In insects, the labium may be very long, may protect the mouthparts, and may serve as a tongue.

nymphs (NIMFS) Young insects that have not yet developed into adults.

order (OR-dur) One kind of group of closely related living things.

parasites (PAR-uh-syts) Creatures that feed on other living things without giving anything back.

predators (PREH-duh-terz) Animals that kill other animals for food.

proboscis (pruh-BAH-sis) Long, sucking mouthparts found on insects, such as bugs, leafhoppers and their relatives, bees, butterflies, and others.

reproductive organs (ree-pruh-DUK-tiv OR-genz) The system inside an animal that allows it to make babies.

saliva (suh-LY-vuh) Liquid in the mouth that starts to break down food.

species (SPEE-sheez) A single kind of plant or animal.

stylets (STY-lets) Long, thin mouthparts made for cutting and for sucking juices.

23

INDEX

WEB SITES

To learn more about assassin bugs, check out these Web sites:
www.enchantedlearning.com/subjects/insects/assassinbug/Assassincolor.shtml
www.uwex.edu/ces/cty/milwaukee/urbanag/bugnet/outwoodies/assassin/
    assassin.html